First
Facts®

OUR
PLACE

T0101159

THE MILKY WAY AND OTHER GALAXIES

by Ellen Labrecque

CAPSTONE PRESS
a capstone imprint

First Facts is published by Capstone
1710 Roe Crest Drive, North Mankato, Minnesota 56003
www.mycapstone.com

Library of Congress Cataloging-in-Publication Data
Names: Labrecque, Ellen, author.
Title: The Milky Way and other galaxies / by Ellen Labrecque.
Description: North Mankato, Minnesota : an imprint of Pebble, [2020] |
    Series: First facts. Our place in the universe | "Pebble is published by
    Capstone." | Audience: Ages 6-9. | Audience: K to grade 3.
Identifiers: LCCN | 2018054592 ISBN 9781977108463 (hardcover) |
    ISBN 9781977110169 (pbk.) | ISBN 978-1977108630 (ebook pdf)
Subjects: LCSH: Galaxies--Juvenile literature. | Milky Way--Juvenile
    literature.
Classification: LCC QB857.3 .L33 2020 | DDC 523.1/13--dc23
LC record available at https://lccn.loc.gov/2018054592

Editorial Credits
Hank Musolf, editor; Kyle Grenz, designer; Jo Miller, media researcher; Kathy McColley, production specialist

Photo Credits
Science Source: European Space Agency, 11, IAP/Yannick Mellier, 17 (Bottom); Shutterstock: AmyLv, 7 (Top Right), enterlinedesign, 7 (Bottom Left), John A Davis, 13, Kaveex, 22, nikm4860, 15 (All), Nolkin, Cover, Paul Stringer, 7 (Top Right), rtguest, 7 (Top Left), Stefano Garau, 21, titoOnz, 5, vectortatu, 18; Wikimedia: NASA & ESA, 19, NASA/JPL-Caltech, 17 (Top), NASA/JPL-Caltech/R. Hurt (SSC/Caltech), 9
Design Elements
Capstone; Shutterstock: Alex Mit, Dimonika, Kanate

All internet sites appearing in back matter were available and accurate when this book was sent to press.

Printed and bound in China.
5174

Table of Contents

Imagine Yourself in Space!

Imagine you are flying through the **universe**. Up! Up! Up! Your home planet Earth looks smaller and smaller. The sun looks like a tiny yellow dot. Stars surround you. They are everywhere! You are in our **galaxy**, the Milky Way.

galaxy—a large group of stars and planets

universe—everything that exists, including Earth, the planets, the stars, and all of space

5

The Milky Way

How big is outer space? You could fly in it for many years and never see it all! Earth is in a solar system. The solar system includes the sun. It also includes seven other planets that travel around it. Our solar system is in the Milky Way galaxy.

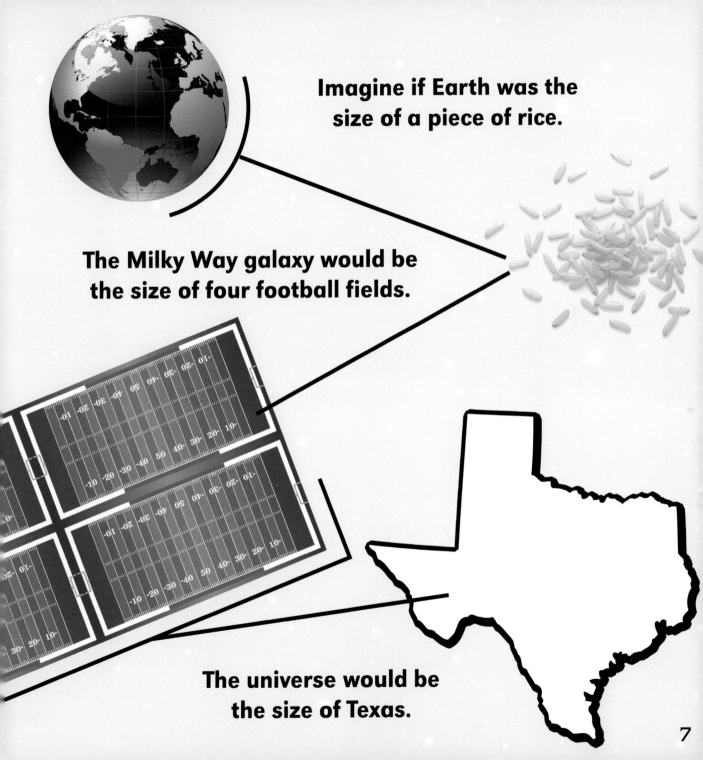

Imagine if Earth was the
size of a piece of rice.

The Milky Way galaxy would be
the size of four football fields.

The universe would be
the size of Texas.

The Milky Way galaxy is shaped like a giant whirlpool. It is made up of billions of stars and planets. It is also made of dust and gas.

Some of the stars are big! They are 100 times bigger than our own sun.

FAR-OUT FACT

There are billions of other galaxies in space.

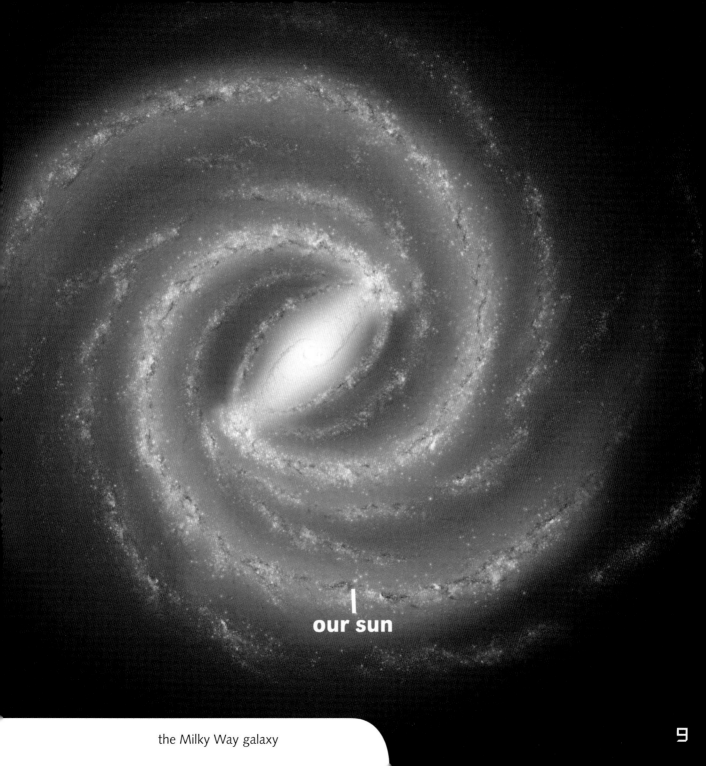

our sun

the Milky Way galaxy

The center of the Milky Way is a giant star that died. It is called a **black hole**. A black hole is like a monster. Its **gravity** sucks anything into it that comes close. It sucks in planets and other stars. It even traps light. That is why it is invisible.

black hole—a star that died

gravity—a force that pulls objects together

a star that collapsed in on itself and now pulls everything nearby into it

The Milky Way galaxy is very big. Scientists can't measure it in miles. They use light-years. The speed of light is the fastest speed we know. In one year, light travels 5.88 trillion miles. It takes light 100,000 years to cross the Milky Way!

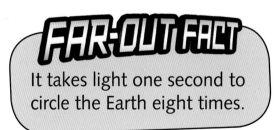

FAR-OUT FACT

It takes light one second to circle the Earth eight times.

light-year—the distance light travels in a year

scientist—a person who studies the world around us

starlight travels very far to reach Earth

Wish upon a Star

A group of stars can look like shapes in the sky. They are called **constellations**. There are 88 constellations in our galaxy. You can look up and see these shapes.

constellation—a group of stars clustered together

Constellations

Here are three famous constellations:

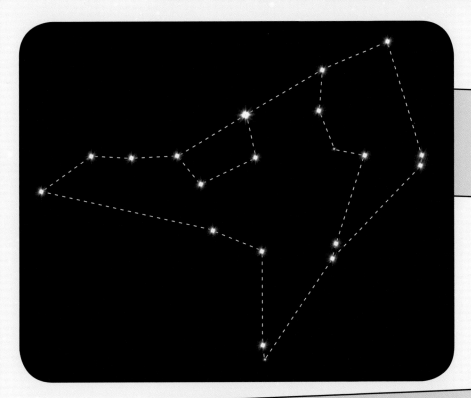

Ursa Major looks like a big bear.

This group of stars is called Orion. It is named after a Greek hunter.

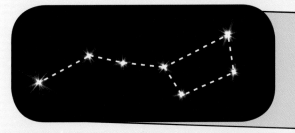

This group of stars is called the Big Dipper. Can you see why?

Other Galaxies

There are billions of galaxies in space. The closest galaxy to the Milky Way is 2.5 million light-years away. It is called the Andromeda galaxy. It is shaped like a spiral. It is much bigger than the Milky Way. It would take light 260,000 years to cross it!

the Andomeda galaxy

drawing of what dark matter might look like

Dark Matter

Scientists believe dark matter is between galaxies. Matter is anything that takes up space. Scientists can't see dark matter with their eyes. It does not give off light or energy. But they still know it is there. They can feel its gravity.

Galaxies come in all shapes and sizes. Spiral galaxies are shaped like pinwheels. Barred spiral galaxies have a long bar in the middle of them.

Types of galaxies

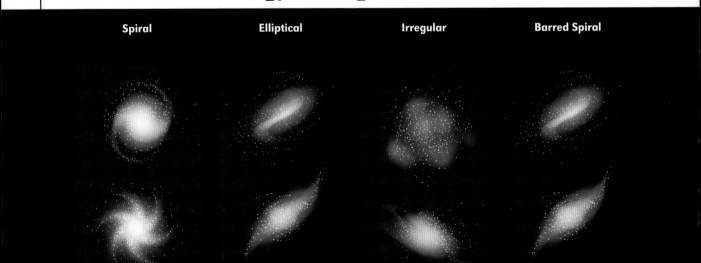

Spiral   Elliptical   Irregular   Barred Spiral

a barred spiral galaxy

Elliptical galaxies are shaped
like discs. They are the oldest type
of galaxy. Irregular galaxies are in
different forms.

Look Up!

Don't forget to look up when you are outside at night. You are looking into the Milky Way. See if you can spot any constellations. Imagine the planets in the distance. The Milky Way is full of wonder!

Glossary

black hole (BLAK HOHL)—a star that collapsed in on itself and now pulls everything nearby into it

constellation (kon-stuh-LAY-shuhn)—a group of stars clustered together

galaxy (GAL-uhk-see)—a large group of stars and planets

gravity (GRAV-i-tee)—a force that pulls objects together

light-year (LITE YEER)—the distance light travels in a year

scientist (SYE-un-tist)—a person who studies the world around us

universe (YOO-nuh-vurs)—everything that exists, including Earth, the stars, and all of space